Into the Mirrored Pool

Lianna Samuel

BookLeaf Publishing

India | USA | UK

Presentation by *BookLeaf Publishing*

Web: www.bookleafpub.com

E-mail: info@bookleafpub.com

ISBN: 9789360949556

First edition 2024

To those who came before and those who come after....

ACKNOWLEDGEMENT

I would like to thank my family, the ones who keep me, build me up and support me always.

PREFACE

We are never alone
Supported by does who came before us
Cheered on by those who stand with us
Encouraged by those who will come after us

Change

Change is hard
We all dread it
But it's always there
Tick, tick, tick
It's hard edge waiting
Like a diamond edged blade
Cutting through moments
Both glad and sad
Slicing and shredding thoughts
Full of happiness and despair
Dicing and destroying days
Filled with sorrow and laughter too
Forcing the bending of our souls
Twisting, turning shifting like sand
Trying to stay in step

Change is inevitable
It is a part of time
Always there
In the background
Like water
Carving through rock
Modifying everything
We trying to stop it
But it bends us

Shapes the world around us
Till the only option
Is to move with it
Bend with it
Just to keep up
And not drown

Change is scary
Of it we are afraid
Seeking to hide
But there is no safe space
It's insidious and deep
Your worst nightmare stuck on repeat
The dream from which you can't awake
Feeling alone in a crowded room
Always one step behind
Forever late with the trend
Invisible even among friends
Lost and confused
Always on edge
Searching for the beat

Change is invincible
We can't stop it
No matter how hard we try
As certain as death and taxes
The perpetual dynamo
What can any of us do
But Just let go

Fall into it, Embrace it
Become one with it
Know that change is both
Internal and external
Building up, breaking down
Reshaping, refining
Evolving our minds

Love in Vain

I can't depend on you
I shouldn't depend on you
And yet I can't seem to remember those two
rules
I depend on you
In vain
Hoping you will help me with my burdens
Catch me when I stumble
Help me be my best for you,
For us,
For the kids
For myself
But you don't
You don't help me
You point out my flaws
My failings
Making me feel less
I'm trying to be better
But I feel lost
And alone
I'm too tired to fight
I'm sad so sad
Asking for help
Gets me nothing
All I'm good for to you is sex

At least that's what it feels like
I'm drowning on my own
But you're there
Watching me
Not saving me
Never reaching out your hand
As I sink to the bottom
And our love dies

Dizzy

Spinning, spinning,
In a continuous loop
Lost in the motion
Too caught up to care
Round and round
Twirl and twist
Spirits dancing with the wind
Circle of life
We are born
Gasping for air
Fresh baby smell
Morning dew on a rose
We grow
Toddling, walking, running
Working, slaving away
We die
Circle of death

Circle of hope
Dreaming, wishing, wanting more
We love
We laugh
We hate
We slight
We are prejudiced

We are imperfect
Circle of despair
Spinning, spinning
In a continuous loop
Orbiting life
Orbiting the sun
Life's a cycle
Sometimes a circus ring
More often than not, a collection of circles

Submitted
Rejected
Use more
Metaphors, On
The flowery platitudes that those who live the
charmed life choose
You words aren't mine
My words aren't yours
If you need rose tinted glasses
To capture the rawness and essence of life
So be it
Don't judge my words
With your need for pretty little sayings
Your need for Onomatopoeia
Imagery and Personification
To describe feelings and life
Why must the raw always be covered
That which you think is ugly changed
Do you turn away from those less fortunate?

Your neighbors in need of help?
Do you ever walk in another's shoes?
Or must it all be prettied just for you?
My life
My experiences
My thoughts
My words
Strong, Concise, Direct
I'm not you
When you review
Do you do so
Standing from you soapbox,
A pedestal where only your way is correct?
Or do you ever read at poetry that is raw
And feel the essence of what is said

Running Away Home

Alone in a crowded room
Bombarded by words and laughter
Too much, too loud, too bright
It feels uncomfortable
Boring beneath my skin
Exhausted, burnt out
Afraid to run
But I must
The oppressiveness blankets me
My voice is lost
Loneliness seeps into me
Awkwardness dragging me down
Depressing me
Slowly inching away
Stepping back
Politely nodding
Agreeing with no idea
Of what I acquiescing to
Blending with the darkness
I turn and flee
Fast and light on my feet
I find what I need
The quiet, the dark
I can breathe, I can be me
The comfort of home

The peacefulness of being alone
No need to feign happiness
No need to entertain
Content to just exist and be

Lost

Misguided
Set adrift by what others say
Confused
Diverted by what others think
We constantly are bombarded
Our own thoughts working against us
Does that fit?
What would the 'in' crowd think?
Society has programmed us
To think of others
Be aware of others
Be silent
Don't step on any toes
Smile and bare it
Be strong
Even if smiling
Means you die a little inside everyday
Hone your strength
Even if it weakens your soul
Conform
Don't make waves
Don't step out of line
Trudge on
Even if as you do so
You lose yourself

How do you break feee?
How do you step into the light?
For so long we've pushed ourselves
Downward to the floor
Groveling at the popular
Making ourselves invisible
Do we even see ourselves?
Our true selves
beyond the reflection in the mirror
Look into your soul
Truly see yourself
See your brilliance
See your beauty
See the potential nestled within
Find that quiet strength inside you
Find your inner muse
And fight
Fight to bring yourself to the surface
Fight to accept how wonderful you are
Fight to find yourself
And no longer be lost

Accept me

Accept me
As I am
Not for what you hope I'll be
Not as the potential you see
Accept me
The imperfect person before you
Sometimes broken
Sometimes strong
Sometimes quiet
Sometimes loud

Accept me
The one who accepts you
Even with your imperfections
Don't try to change me
Change must come from an internal force
Don't force your opinions on me
We are different
Who we are
Where we've come from our experiences
But in those differences we are the same

Accept me
Knowing that I am constantly working
Striving to be better

Growing with each new experience
Evolving as a person
Fitting into my skin
Gaining confidence in who I am

Accept me
As I learn to accept myself
My experiences
The past that shaped me
The present that pushes me
The hope that inspires me

Accept me
Just like this
So when I 'm down
I know there's someone in my corner

Enough

I am enough
You are enough
We are all enough
We are all of worth
As much as is required
To make a difference
In our own small part of the world

We are all unique
One of a kind
No one can duplicate
Our experiences
Our emotions
Our reactions
Are unlike any other

The amazing creation
That is us
No one can replace us
Our kindness
Our hope
Our faith
We each make a small ripple

We each make a difference

We make friends
We love
We make an impact
No matter how small
To those we meet
We impact their world.

Luck

A series of events
Connected or not
Serendipity
Coincidence
Karma
Fate
Supersition
A four leaf clover
A horseshoe
Rabbit's foot
Lucky penny
Dreamcatcher
Driven by thought of the unknown
How do I increase my chances?
Improve my luck?
Do we control our own luck?
Through our actions
Our words

Harmony

Music is everywhere
Close your eyes
The drip of water
From the tap to the kettle
The rumble of excited water molecules
As the kettle heats up
Speeding up in cadence
Growing louder and louder
Until the crescendo of the steam whistling
Close your eyes
Let your mind drift to your favorite place
The sounds that envelop you there
The ocean
The rhythmic crashing of the waves
The crunch of the sand beneath the feet
The rush of the surf as it surges and retreats
The forest
The wind whistling through the trees
The sounds on feet on leaves
The crunch when dry the squelch when wet
The pitter patter of the rain hitting the leaves
The rush of the distant waterfall
Home
wrapped up cozy in a blanket
The roar of heavy rainfall on a metal roof

A warm embrace
The beating of two hearts
Words of comfort
Sweet nothings in an ear
Companionable silence

Exhale

Find the calm
The balance
Of enjoying the present
No worries about I the past
No doubts about the future
Just embracing the now
Find the grace to accept yourself
As you are
Not wishing to be anyone else
No Reminiscing on how you were
No hoping on what you'll be
Find the peace
In letting go
Of Everyone else's expectations
Of pleasing the masses
Just be
The beautiful amazing person
That you are

Hot Swirl Paint

Imagine hot swirled paint
The pulsing mystic
The paint that glows
Flowing from within
Outward through your aura
Letting light in
Embracing others
Swirling around those you touch
The essence of you
Transmitted
Through every thought
Every single action
Every word you speak
Whether colored
Hot oranges or reds
Filled with anger, passion and pain
Quickly drawing
Harsh and stinging
Misery seeking company
Cool blues and greens
Icy frosty
Unwilling to bend
Unflinchingly straight
ghosting those who feel your disdain
Keeping your heart safe

Warm and neutral
As you drift by
Accepting that everything has its own time
Letting go of things
That don't bring you pride
Take a chance
in loving yourself
Who you were
Who you are
Who you will be

Love is

A warm embrace
Wrapped in a thick
Lush blanket
That caresses your skin
Massages your scalp
Sending tingles along your head
Racing down your spine
A kind word
Stroking your face
Filling your brain
With soothing vibrations

Everything

All the riches
All of the treasures
Everything in this world
Is just a tiny speck
In the universe
A minuscule amount of
The vastness
All of the exotic
All of the unusual
Everything in this word
Is fleeting
Just one moment
In the millennia
A tiny fraction of
The endless
All of the seconds
All of the touches
Everything in this world
Spent with you
Is unbounded
Filling the heart
Overflowing with the joy
Of your presence
Flushed with the happiness
Of your love

Fexible

Find your center!
Focus
Breathe, Stretch
Move your body.
Contort and flex.
Feel the tightness loosen.
The stress release.

Find your purpose.
Adapt
Change, evolve and grow.
Every day, a new adventure
A chance to do.
To become
To achieve

Flexibility is a boon.
Adaptability a revered trait
To excel in this world
You need to be up for a change.

Recipe

What is a recipe?
A group of ingredients
Items that should go together,
Things that when combined
Produce
Delightful smells
Scrumptious feasts

Substitutions?
Could be hit or miss,
To make it work
You need to think things through.
Texture
Taste
Sugar content

A set of instructions
To be followed step by step
Read it once and then again
Don't hurry too much
You might miss a step.
Then what to do?
A quick fix
or start over again.

Whether you choose
To start simple
Or complex
Believe in your ability!
Gather everything you need.
Try your best.
You will succeed

Resolve uncrushed.

Use more Metaphors,
Oh, such flowery platitudes.
That those who live the charmed life choose.
Your words aren't mine
My words aren't yours
If you need rose tinted glasses
To capture the rawness and essence of life
So be it,
Don't judge my words.
With your need for pretty-little sayings
Your need for Onomatopoeia
Imagery and Personification
To describe feelings and life
Why must raw emotion always be covered?
And that which you think is ugly changed.
Do you turn away from those less fortunate?
Your neighbors in need of help?
Do you ever walk in another's shoes?
Or must it all be prettied just for you?
My life
My experiences
My thoughts
My words
Strong, Concise, Direct
I'm not you.

When you review
You stand upon your soapbox,
A pedestal where only your way is correct?
Or do you ever read poetry that is raw?
And feel the essence of what is unsaid.

Shades

Shades, blinds
Covers for windows
Keeping out the sun
Keeping out prying eyes
Protecting secrets
Keeping us safe

Shades, Sunglasses
Covers for the eyes
Windows to the soul
Keeping outsiders
Away from our thoughts
Keeping thoughts hidden

Shades provide protection
From others
From ourselves
They lull us
into false safety

Sometimes
It's best
to remove the shades
To let the world in
It may surprise you

Sea bound

The sounds
Waves crashing
Surf running up the sand
The smells
Seaweed washed ashore
Fresh fish hauled in nets
The sight

Rich blue
Turquoise
Sea-Green
Deceptively calm
Or Tumultuous
Roiling with waves
Hidden currents

A fisherman's boom
Or curse
A place of calm
For families to enjoy
Children to splash
For scientist to discover
So much left to uncover

The beauty is corrupted

By invisible aliens
Ever present
Impossible to remove
Tiny pieces of plastic
in the waterways
In the food chain
Micro-embedded

Dingolay

Heavy beats
Loud instrumentation
Swelling emotions
Passionate intensity
Churning feelings
Releasing pent up rage
Quelling the volcano within

Smooth, sweet, soft melodies
Caressing the soul
Touching the mind
Bringing joy
Soothing pain
Like a balm
Healing ancient wounds

Haunting melodies
Evokes lingering sadness
Poignant lyrics
Producing Melancholy
Driving Introspection
Lifting despair
From your soul

Gentle rhythms

Provide relaxing relief
Calming and true
Lightening the spirit
Lulling one to sleep
Decompressing
Relieving stress

Sweet tones, fast energy
Trigger happiness
Warming the heart
Celebrating life
Loves, Friendships,
Remembrances of fetes

No matter the melody
The rhythm or beat
Music fuels the soul
Feeds the mind
Enlivens the heart
Moves the body
To dingolay

Puzzle Pieces

It's amazing
How well we mesh
From distant homes
So different and yet ...
Your hand holding mine
Just feels right

The joy of being me
Increases when I'm with you you
You accept me as I am
No need to change
No need to be anything else
You make me feel special,
Loved for who I am
With you
I never have to pretend

You get me
I get you too
Your quirks
Your idiosyncrasies
Make you human
And more special to me
I don't want to change you
I enjoy every moment we share

This must be love
Our give and take
Accepting each other
Growing together
Comforting each other
Being together
Made for each other

TLC

Sometimes when least expected
And the world seems dismal and gray
Happiness happens
On thought
One memory
Produces a smile
An almost imperceptible change

In the silence, frustrated and lonely
Watching the room's walls cave in
Bliss begins
A melody
A lyric
Bestows hope
Gently enlightening the spirit

Late whilst, over worked, tired, stressed
Feeling unworthy and insignificant
Ecstacy enters
One texture
One image
Fuels the mind
Placing everything in perspective

At the lowest, weakest, frailest moment

When self-doubt and night time shadows
Overpower what little strength is left
Joy floods the soul
Lifting up beyond despair
Giving that which is missed the most
Tender Loving Care